# AN UPGRADER'S
# GUIDE

## HOW TO MOVE ON FROM CHRISTIANITY
## & REDISCOVER JESUS

For David –

with admiration

and affection,

# F. HUGH MAGEE

ISBN: 0615337635
ISBN-13: 9780615337630

*... the truth as it is in Jesus.*
Ephesians 4:21 [NEB]

# ACKNOWLEDGEMENTS

All the ideas that follow are inspired by the thought system presented in *A Course in Miracles.* However, while these ideas are not my own, their expression here is generally mine (except when attributed to others) and I also accept responsibility for any comments about the Course itself in the latter part of this book. Although I would thus not wish to hold others accountable for any aspect of what I have written, I should acknowledge the supportive input of family members and numerous individuals on both sides of the Atlantic who have heard or read many of the ideas presented in this book in incipient form in various settings.

I would also like to express my thanks to a number of individuals who have assisted this project with their wise counsel and specific help. I begin with Lewis Lapham, then Editor of *Harper's Magazine*, for his early and helpful support. Later, two colleagues from Westcott House, Cambridge, who, although they have not specifically endorsed what I have written, were nevertheless among the first to encourage this project (or something like it): The Reverend Don Cupitt, Emeritus Professor of the University of Cambridge, and The Right Reverend Michael Hare Duke, sometime Bishop of St. Andrews. I would also like to express my gratitude to The Right Reverend Richard Holloway, formerly Bishop of Edinburgh and Primus of the Scottish Episcopal Church, for likewise encouraging my work at an early stage and making some specific suggestions. (Although Bishop Holloway has since read this book in manuscript form and referred to it as "intriguing stuff", he has not found himself able to embrace its content.)

I have in fact submitted this book in manuscript form to a number of Anglican bishops and I am grateful to the Right Reverend James Waggoner, Bishop of Spokane, and the Right Reverend John Spong, sometime Bishop of Newark, for their favourable comments.

Special thanks are due to my friends at CreateSpace for their invaluable assistance in preparing this book for publication; and to Dr. Kenneth Wapnick, Director of The Foundation for *A Course in Miracles,* for his encouragement and his willingness to undertake a detailed review of this material and suggest one or two small (though important) corrections. I also thank Jon Mundy, Publisher of *Miracles Magazine,* and Tom Gossett, the former editor of the *Insight* newsletter, for their valued suggestions.

I must express particular gratitude to Diane Egby-Edwards, of Bournemouth, for making specific suggestions about the form and nature of what follows. The fact that this book was written at all is in fact largely due to her valuable counsel and hypnotherapeutic skills.

But it is my wife Yvonne whom I must thank most of all for the fact that this material ever reached fruition in published form. She has been both my most constructive critic and my most faithful supporter as I have sought to complete this project.

Finally, it would be remiss not to acknowledge the essential role played by Helen Schucman and William Thetford, late Professors of Medical Psychology at Columbia University's College of Physicians and Surgeons in New York City, and co-scribes of *A Course in Miracles*. Without their "little willingness" to provide us with these teachings, this book could not have been conceived at all. Thank you, Helen & Bill.

F.H.M.
St. Andrews, Scotland
Ascensiontide, 2010

# PREFACE

If you're wondering what this book is about, you deserve an explanation.

Our thesis here is three-fold:

1) That Christianity is obsolete
2) That we therefore need to move on to a better Jesus-inspired thought system
3) That such a thought system is now available

While there are many voices today that would consent to the first of these three statements, or something like it, we do not receive much help with the second, while the third is largely unknown.

The reason for this is simple: it's much easier to diagnose a problem than to solve it.

Yet today we have at our disposal a means by which the problem of Christian dysfunction can be solved in a way that is entirely compatible with the mind of Jesus.

My present purpose is to help people to upgrade to that solution.

Please note that we are concerned here solely with theological dysfunction. It is not my intention to denigrate whatever benefits may have been received and shared through the medium of Christianity in the past, or even today. Christian communities have been a blessing to many people through the ages and one would not wish to deny this. Nor would one wish to overlook the many 'Christian' efforts to alleviate the world's material needs that have been a mark of Christianity at its best from its inception. The value of such efforts is normally beyond dispute and they have largely been true reflections of the 'social gospel' of Jesus.

Indeed, one would not forget what Karen Armstrong has called "the spirit of compassion that lies at the core of all of our traditions".

Finally, this book is not intended to be an attack on the Church, though it is likely to be perceived as such. Rather, it is written "with love to the Church", to borrow a title from the late Monica Furlong.

And above all, Jesus remains at the very heart of the enterprise.

# CONTENTS

N.B. In this text, British spelling and punctuation norms are preferred. Please also note that, in accordance with some international practice, single quotation marks have been employed to set off certain words as they are used in common parlance – e.g. 'sin'.

# INTRODUCTION

For the past two millennia, the belief system that has dominated much of Western civilization has been Christianity. Today there are more Christians alive than ever before, comprising about a third of the world's population, and this growth will likely continue well into the 21st century.

Yet despite its seeming success, adherence to Christianity has declined markedly among educated people during the past century and most of its current growth has taken place in what is now referred to (rather sweepingly) as the 'Global South'. As a result, many of today's new Christians live in countries that are not Christian by tradition. One result of this is that the theology so embraced tends to be somewhat undeveloped and, despite their frequent willingness to defend 'biblical truth', the new adherents often have little real understanding of the Bible, its complexity and its origins.

At the same time, in the so-called Christian nations of Europe and North America, pluralism has become a norm in cultures that were once considered 'Christian', while the number of 'practicing' Christians is in sharp decline, particularly in Europe. While not denying that there are some who still benefit from Christianity as traditionally presented, the fastest-growing segment of potential seekers is made up of those who, though they may admire Jesus and what they perceive to be his liberal attitude to life, have become disillusioned with credal forms of Christianity. Though not specifically religious, they continue to seek meaning and personal integrity, with Jesus serving as a kind of reference point.

No doubt indicative of this trend, a number of voices (Sam Harris, Richard Dawkins, Christopher Hitchens and others), speaking today in the tradition of Spinoza and Bertrand Russell, have been critical, not just of Christianity, but of *all* religions. While there may be nothing new in this, the fact that the work of such writers has generated a number of contemporary best sellers perhaps speaks for itself.

Meanwhile, Christendom as such is becoming increasingly conflicted and confused, allowing its credibility to be eroded (at least among thinking people) by meaningless debates about issues that are of little or no concern to society as a whole (does it really matter whether or not Jesus was married?). Moreover, those who would propose 'Christian' solutions to more pressing problems (population control perhaps being the most urgent) are often hopelessly out of their depth in dealing with such matters as medical ethics and human sexuality. So often the Christian 'witness' is in fact unhelpful – when straight answers are attempted, they tend to be misleading at best and at worst, simply wrong.

In fact, again and again the Christian influence has been more a part of the problems it would address than of their solution (though this can often be said of other religions as well).

In a word, Christian dysfunction is now manifest on every hand and, despite a continuation of its outward success, Christianity as we have known it seems to be dying a slow death from within.

---
**Christianity as we have known it seems to be dying a slow death from within.**

---

But if Christianity has ever stood for anything at all, it has been the truth that out of apparent death comes resurrection.

In practice, it is the function of theological evolution to help us to move beyond the empty tomb and "meet Jesus again for the first time", in the words of Marcus Borg.

Yet it is also the thesis of this book that Jesus is likewise *meeting us again* today in what I can only call a 'Second Coming'.

What this means is that the time has come for us to move on from Christianity and rediscover Jesus.

# PRELIMINARY STUFF

*Check your premises.*
**Ayn Rand**

# PROLOGUE

In light of the present confusion that prevails in the worldwide Christian community, it's perhaps not surprising that many thinking people have abandoned formal Christianity, while remaining committed to a search for God or, at least, meaning. Although repelled by many aspects of the religion with which he has become associated, they would yet retain Jesus as an icon of truth.

Before we can hope to move on from Christianity to a rediscovery of Jesus, it might therefore be helpful to address some of the issues that lie behind the present confusion.

In fact, there are certain key ideas that obviously need to be clarified if we are to avoid getting entangled in pointless arguments about, say, the authority of the Bible or the divinity of Jesus.

So let's start with some of the high profile stuff.

# GOD IS

Let's begin with 'God', which is the term we use to denote Ultimate Reality.

The most important thing we need to know about God is that "God is".

Actually, that's about all we *can* know about God, since That which we think we are referring to when we use this word is the ultimate Mystery.

What this means is that although the idea of God is arguably the highest thought our minds can seek, it "exceeds our grasp", to borrow a well-known phrase from the poet Robert Browning.

Virtually all of our religious problems arise, not from the idea of God as such, but from our assumptions *about* that idea, which are inevitably based on the fantasy that we can "grasp" What God is.

But in reality, virtually everything we say about God must of necessity take the form of a symbol or metaphor.

When you come right down to it, the term 'God' is itself a kind of metaphor and even people who identify themselves as non-believers or 'atheists' still have to buy into it to some extent before they can try to explain what it is they think they don't believe in!

It's OK to use all the metaphors we want for God, so long as we remember that these cannot *define* God – they are only metaphors: symbols of a symbol, if you like.

---

**It's OK to use all the metaphors we want for God, so long as we remember that these cannot *define* God – they are only metaphors: symbols of a symbol, if you like.**

---

The best such modern symbol may well be the one proposed in the last century by the great theologian, Paul Tillich. He referred to God as "the ground of all being".

According to the Bible, when Jesus talked about God, he used the metaphor "Father", so you could say that this one has a pretty sound pedigree.

Another useful metaphor for God, which is also in the Bible, lies in the statement that "God is Light". This is a good one to use because it expresses the all-encompassing nature of That to which we are referring.

The metaphor of Light is likewise apt today since it works well with the "light energy" associated with quantum mechanics.

It's also one that we can identify with more personally if we allow ourselves to think of God as a kind of energy Source that we can tap into (and of Which we are a part).

All this of course has some implications for the way we pray. For example, how does one identify in prayer with "the ground of all being"? (More on this later.)

The problem with most religion is that it makes the mistake of confusing the metaphors we inevitably need to use for God with That to which they refer.

There's only one metaphor that really gets around this problem. It does so by bridging the gap between God and our own experience. We find this one in the Bible as well – in fact, it's the most important statement in the entire Bible.

It's the simple affirmation that "God is Love" (I John 4:8, 16b).

What makes this particular metaphor so powerful is that it really expresses the only truth we'll ever need to know about God (or anything else, for that matter) in this world or the next – the Beatles were right about that.

This metaphor is so close to the ultimate reality we call 'God' that it can be applied without reservation, not least since love itself (whether human or divine) cannot be known *except* in relationship.

If you want to know what the metaphor of Love means when we apply it to relationship with God, read the Parable of the Loving Father (popularly called the Parable of the Prodigal Son) in the Gospel of Luke (Luke 15:11-32) – it's all there.

By the way, it's also OK to think of God as Creator (through the extension of Love), so long as we don't allow that metaphor to get us into senseless arguments about science vs. religion.

But all attempts to conceive of God as anything but Love should be discarded – and the sooner the better.

---

**All attempts to conceive of God as anything but Love should be discarded – and the sooner the better.**

---

# THE HOLY SPIRIT
# AS 'VOICE' FOR GOD

As I suggested in the last section, the fact that What we think we are referring to when we use the word 'God' is ultimately beyond our comprehension does not mean that we can't relate to It.

Happily, we can bridge the gap between our limited human understanding and the unlimited energy we call God by means of a 'Holy Spirit'.

This Holy Spirit can (and does) provide us with a direct connection with God while we are living in bodies.

There will come a time when we will no longer need to bridge the seeming gap between our identity and the ultimate energy of God because we will have fully remembered who we are. When that happens, we will know again that there *is* no gap.

But until that happens we need the Holy Spirit to remind us that who we are is actually no different from What God is.

This is good news since it means that the only problem we think we have – the belief that we have somehow become separate from our Source – is no more than a human illusion.

---

**The only problem we think we have – the belief that we have somehow become separate from our Source – is no more than a human illusion.**

---

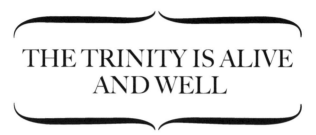

# THE TRINITY IS ALIVE AND WELL

Baffled by Christian dogma that tells us that God is manifest in "three persons", traditionally understood as "Father, Son and Holy Spirit"?

Well, don't be. It's just a kind of three-fold mantra or training aid that Christians like to use when referring to God.

And if it doesn't work for you, you can scrap it.

Or, better still, tweak it, as the Church itself has done from time to time.

For example, some contemporary liturgies have modified the traditional formula in such a way as to make it seem less remote.

But no matter how it is expressed, visualizing God as 'three in one' can be a helpful way of making sure that, in our approach to the Mystery of God, nothing from our existing experience and knowledge is left out.

So this seemingly baffling dogma can have its uses.

For example, it can help us to unpack the idea of God a bit in our minds so it's more user-friendly.

After all, although as we've said the concept of God is the highest thought our minds can seek, it's essentially incomprehensible as a human idea.

So we may need some help getting our minds around it a bit, so to speak.

To put it another way, the Truth of which the idea of God is a symbol is so powerful that It can literally blow our minds. So we may need to find some ways to lower the voltage.

If so, you could think of the idea (that's all it is, by the way) of the Trinity as a kind of electrical transformer that can help us to process the concept of God by breaking it down a bit.

---

**The idea of the Trinity can help us to process the concept of God by breaking it down a bit.**

---

Actually, this dumbing down of Truth (as a cynic might call it) is all what we think of as 'religion' is really about anyway. What this means is that religious ideas and formulas are always up for grabs.

So we can *reinterpret* the idea of the Trinity if we find it more confusing than helpful.

For example, the idea that Jesus is the "only Son of God" is just plain silly!

# THE CHURCH IS
# NOT THE PROBLEM

It's tempting to blame the Church for Christian dysfunction and to conclude that we should therefore let it die a natural death.

But the Church is not the problem. After all, as a wise priest once said, there's nothing wrong with the Church that can't be fixed – the real problem is obsolete belief.

---

**There's nothing wrong with the Church that can't be fixed.**

---

So (with apologies to Shakespeare) let's not shoot the messenger; let's clean up the message.

After all, since the Church, like everything else in this world, was (in a phrase attributed to Jesus) "made for man", it's a purely human invention, operating with varying degrees of good intent, and sometimes to good effect (in helping to provide a Western alternative to Communism and Fascism, for example).

The fact that it is in constant need of reform simply bears witness to its temporal and fallible nature.

Yet the truth is, we need religious institutions. Without them, we would have no shared symbols for God to help light our way — "to keep the rumour of God alive", as the saying goes.

Without the Church, for example, there would be no recognized symbol for God as revealed by Jesus.

And besides that, who would bury us when we die and all that?

And who would be society's non-political conscience?

It's true that the Church often supports some crazy ideas ('original sin', for example), but that can all be fixed.

And if we didn't have the Church, someone would invent a new equivalent anyway (nature abhors a vacuum).

And that might lead to some form of totalitarianism.

True, the Church itself has been totalitarian for much of its history, but it has also shown itself to be capable of reform and renewal – of reinventing itself, if you like.

So, as Hilaire Belloc once advised, though in a rather different context: "Always keep a hold of nurse, for fear of meeting something worse!"

Let's keep the Church, then, but upgrade from its obsolete belief system.

Or, better still, let Jesus do so because to our minds he's the only one who has the authority to get away with it!

# LET'S NOT WORSHIP JESUS

In a city where I once lived, local parish churches liked to display a cheerful banner which read as follows:

One Church, one Lord
JESUS CHRIST
Worship him here!

This is nonsense.

What's the point of worshipping Jesus?

To worship Jesus is actually to make him irrelevant by suggesting that he's somehow different from the rest of us. That would make it virtually impossible to follow his example.

But the only difference between Jesus and us is that he *got it*.

What he got was that he and the Father were one — that's why he could call God "Father" in the first place!

In other words, he remembered that he was God's 'Son', as we all are.

People who get it (and Jesus hasn't been the only one) are bearers of the Light in a world of darkness. Because all the world's darkness arises from a belief in the impossible: that we have somehow become separated from our Source (what we call 'God').

As the Anglican monk Harry Williams once put it: "All evil consists of my refusal to believe in what I truly am, that I and the Father are one."

---

**"All 'evil' consists of my refusal to believe in what I truly am, that I and the Father are one."**

---

Realize this and you're free.

Of course, we still need to work at it, even if it takes more than one lifetime. But Jesus and other bearers of the Light are available to help us speed up the process.

And, conveniently for us, living in this age of information technology, we now have all the data we need to do just that (more on this later on).

So let's not insult Jesus by worshipping him – instead, let's listen to him!

And, by so doing, put ourselves on the fast track.

To remembering who *we* are.

# THE BIBLE IS NOT THE WORD OF GOD

Perhaps the most incredible concept the Church has ever come up with is the notion that the Bible is somehow the "Word of God".

This magical idea has probably done more harm to the human race than anything except religion itself!

Even in religious terms it's idolatrous since it allows something that is of human origin (i.e. an idol) to take the place of God, a confusion that is itself forbidden in the most familiar version of the 10 Hebrew Commandments (Exodus 20:1-17).

It also trivializes the idea of God by seeming to imply that He (sic) uses words!

Of course, the usual explanation is that it's not the words as such but the Bible as a whole that's the "Word" of God. Yet if this were true (which, thank God, it is not) it would amount to an open invitation to atheism for many thinking people, since the Bible includes so much misinformation (e.g. the popular fiction that Jesus died for our sins).

But God is not mocked by such means. Nor can the Bible be devalued in such a way. It's too important a book for that.

For example, would we have even heard of Jesus if there were no Bible?

In fact, until now the Bible has been an invaluable documentary source. Without it we would not have had access to a collection of writings that, no matter how imperfectly, share a single purpose: seeking to declare the reality of God.

It has done so by means of myth, oracle, history, narrative, poetry, teaching and fantasy.

It's also important to recognize that, as with all great art, there are parts of this collection that are undoubtedly inspired. For example, it would be absurd to suggest that the 23$^{rd}$ Psalm is any less inspired than Mozart's *Requiem* or Michelangelo's sculpture of David.

The fact that the Bible's high purpose of upholding the reality of God was imperfectly achieved in no way diminishes its value as a document of immense importance, both in terms of preserving a given spiritual tradition and inspiring many millions of people for thousands of years.

Remember that the Holy Spirit can and does use *anything* (even religion) to get through to us – and it doesn't have to be perfect.

So don't knock the Bible.

But don't overestimate it either. After all, contrary to popular belief, the Bible has no real authority at all – it's just a resource.

---

**The Bible has no real authority at all – it's just a resource.**

---

You might think of it as a frame.

Happily, thanks to Jesus, we now have a picture to put in the frame (more on this later on).

# MOVING ON FROM CHRISTIANITY

*When people cease to experience God, they are forced to believe in Him …*
**Stephan Hoeller**

# PROLOGUE

Now that we have cleared away some of the under-brush, so to speak, let's take a look at Christian belief itself.

My purpose in the following section of this book is to challenge some of the key assumptions that under-lie Christian orthodoxy as such. While it is recognized that one of the characteristics of 'orthodoxy' is that it in fact *develops*, as Cardinal Newman came to see in the 19th century, we are concerned here mainly with the form of Christianity that began to emerge in the fourth century C.E.

# GOD DOESN'T 'DO' ANYTHING!

In order to move on from Christianity (or, for that matter, any religion) it's essential at the outset that we avoid throwing out the baby with the bath water, so to speak.

So let's begin with an agreed assumption that there is an ultimate reality we call 'God'.

Because without this idea, there wouldn't be a Christianity for us to move on *from*.

Beginning with the idea of God isn't as simple as it might sound, though, because of the baggage that usually goes with it.

As we said in the opening section of this book, virtually all of our religious problems arise, not from the idea of God as such, but from our ideas *about* that idea.

There's a very simple reason for this: while thoughts *about* God are of human origin, the idea *of* God itself is not – it's like a kind of memory chip that we were all born with, even though we may be totally unaware of it at a conscious level.

What this means is that although we all have a built-in capacity to 'know' God, the *idea* of God as such is, as we've said, essentially beyond our comprehension, which is why it's best referred to as a *mystery*.

As long as we stick with the idea of God as mystery we're on secure ground. The trouble starts when we try to unravel the mystery by seeking to define God, describe God, or otherwise allow our human belief systems to make God in our own image.

So let's begin our beginning by making a very clear distinction between the idea of God and our ideas *about* that idea; because it's only the latter that need concern us.

It's essential that we make this distinction at the outset because, although the idea of God itself is the highest Truth our minds can seek, our ideas about that idea are invariably distorted.

---

**Although the idea of God is the highest Truth our minds can seek, our ideas about that idea are invariably distorted.**

---

In other words, believing in God is one thing, but believing all the hype about God (i.e. religion) is quite another.

As a kind of caveat, it might be helpful to make a further distinction between religion and mysticism, which is the direct experience of That which God is.

Although this experience is utterly non-transferable it can and does inspire art and liturgy. It also changes lives.

We call people who have these direct experiences (Francis of Assisi, John Wesley, etc.) 'mystics' because they have begun to penetrate the mystery of God – they have come to know God directly.

The only genuine goal of religion is to make us *all* mystics.

The irony is that, once this has begun to happen, our need for religion will begin to lessen, though we can of course still enjoy liturgy, religious art and ritual, valuing them as attempts to give permanent form to the experience of the Mystery of God.

As for religion as such, its real function is to help us to replace form with content, and by so doing, make us *less religious!*

---

**The real function of religion is to help us to replace form with content, and by so doing, make us *less religious!*

---

Fortunately for us, becoming less religious is easier than we might think. All we need to do is replace our ideas *about* God with the experience *of* God.

While this process, like learning to ride a bike, is likely to take time, it can be done. And you could say that religion is like a set of training wheels to get us going in the right direction.

In the meantime, let's stop thinking of God as a Being Who does stuff or makes demands. God doesn't do any of that.

But if not, what is God 'for'?

Happily, Jesus has given us all the information we really need on this. What Jesus tells us is that the Bible is right about at least one thing: "God is Love" (I John 4:8,16b). Now we've already touched on the idea of Love as the only metaphor for God we can trust. Whoever wrote it down before it found its way into the Bible evidently wanted to make sure we got the point, since he or she said it twice.

But while Jesus agrees with the Bible when it says God is Love, he takes this idea further by stating that God is *nothing else!*

What this means is that none of the other things people have claimed God to be over the centuries — lawgiver, judge, punisher, sugar daddy, etc. — are true or valid.

In fact, God doesn't really *do* anything. As we've said, God merely *is*. (If you think about it, the concept of 'doing' is a purely human idea anyway.)

But if all that is so, how on earth are we supposed to pray?

The answer to that actually lies in the words "on earth". As long as we live on earth we perceive ourselves as being separate from our Source. Prayer is a way of healing that perception.

Many people think this includes asking for things we want from God and, according to Jesus, that's OK. But after a while we will realize that ultimately, it doesn't work. The reason for this is that we don't actually *know* what we want. Once we realize this, it frees us up to encounter the knowledge that all we *really* want is God.

If we go on from there, seeking God in prayer, the time will come when we will become aware of the fact that since we are made in the image of God, God isn't just someplace else, but *within us.*

When that happens, our prayer is likely to become more like a meditation of some kind. (As you may have noticed, meditation is big these days.)

There's one important exception to the fact that God doesn't actually do anything, however, which we also mentioned earlier: God *creates.*

Contrary to popular religion, however, this has nothing to do with 'creationism'.

Jesus straightens us out on this as well when he tells us that the way God creates is by extending Love. This extension is without limit or exception and it imposes no conditions and makes no demands.

We can't of course fully understand what any of that means, but we can enter into the same creative process ourselves.

We do it whenever we ourselves extend unconditional Love.

In fact, since we are "made in the image of God," it's in our nature to do this and, as God's creation, it's our only task.

For Love is what we are.

# LOVE IS THE ONLY
# REALITY

There's another thing we really need to know before we can outgrow Christianity.

It's essential that we learn this because everything else depends on it.

In fact, our rediscovery of Jesus won't really happen at all until we learn it.

Actually, it has less to do with learning, than with *un*-learning or discarding.

What we need to discard is our belief in opposites.

Now admittedly this belief has been around for a long time and it certainly wasn't a Christian invention. In fact, we can read about it in the second creation narrative in the book of Genesis (Genesis 2:5-3:24), which focuses on the destiny of the human race, as represented by the symbolic figures of Adam & Eve.

As we all know, in this second story of creation – which, by the way, is quite different from the first

(Genesis 1:1-2:4) – Adam & Eve eat the forbidden fruit of the tree of the knowledge of good and evil. And that, according to the story, is how all the trouble started: we somehow bought into the idea of good and evil.

Now the problem with believing that good and evil exist as opposites is that these terms don't really mean anything, except to the people who use them. In other words, their definition depends on how they are applied.

So, for example, while some might regard suicide bombers as good (i.e. heroes or martyrs), others will see them as evil (i.e. murderers and terrorists).

Because of ambiguities like these, it's best to avoid the ideas of good and evil and find a more helpful terminology.

It's better to think in terms of Love and fear: not only are these terms more precise, but they denote the only apparent opposites we really need to deal with.

Doing so is greatly simplified by the fact that there's a qualitative difference between Love and fear: Love reflects that which is real, while fear is based on nothing.

The reason for this is quite simple. If God is Love (and as we've said, according to Jesus, that's *all* God is) that means that Love, like God, must be all-encompassing.

If that is so, then there can be no real opposite to Love, since God can have no opposite that actually exists – to suggest that God can have an opposite that's real is in fact a form of disbelief in God because it seeks to limit That which has no limit.

In a word, *Love is all there is.*

Since there's no opposite to Love, fear has no basis.

Thus to believe in fear is to believe in nothing.

Since all of our judgements reflect a belief in evil (or fear) they are actually based on nothing.

While Love is based on everything.

The choice between Love and fear is therefore a choice between everything and nothing.

---

## The choice between Love and fear is a choice between everything and nothing.

---

Whether we realize it or not, we are making this choice all the time. In fact there are no other options available.

Our only task is to replace fear with Love in every situation.

And by so doing, move from nothing to everything.

How can we do it?

Fortunately, Jesus has passed on the secret – it's even in the Bible: "Perfect Love casts out fear" (I John 4:18)

This is really all we need to know if we would be happy and sane.

# THERE IS NO SIN

If God creates only by extending Love and if that extension makes no demands and imposes no conditions, it follows that the popular notion of 'sin' is a purely human invention — it has nothing to do with God, in other words.

In fact, we get ourselves into real trouble if we try to involve God in what we perceive to be our imperfections.

Because doing so will put us on the fast track to guilt.

And guilt is a killer, for sure.

True, there's a lot about sin in the Bible. But almost all of it reflects such fantasies as the incredible notion that God punishes sin. The only biblical idea on the subject that avoids this kind of mistake is the one that refers to sin as a falling short of the mark (as in archery).

Yet even that image can lead us astray if it suggests to us that God is somehow watching to see where the arrows are landing!

So it's best if we just abandon the toxic notion of sin altogether.

And for our mental health, it's absolutely essential that we avoid the fatal mistake of confusing sins to be punished (false) with mistakes to be corrected (true).

Before we can move on from Christianity, therefore, we need to make this crucial distinction between falsehood and truth.

That task is made much easier once we accept the fact that, as we've said, God doesn't actually 'do' anything except create through the extension of Love.

This idea is worth repeating since it leads to a realization that God does not judge, God does not condemn, and God does not punish – never has, never will.

But if sins go unpunished, does that mean that 'anything goes' and everyone can do as they like?

Strictly speaking, that's true. But to leave it at that would be to overlook the fact that we're still accountable for everything we think and do.

So consider this: we live in a universe that operates according to the law of cause and effect, what the biblical writers sometimes called "sowing and reaping".

What that means is that what we're putting out is exactly what we'll get back.

Crudely put, this idea appears to echo the Old Testament's rather scary legal prescription of "an eye for an eye and a tooth for a tooth". But the law works both ways, as suggested by the more positive teaching attributed to Jesus in the New Testament: "The measure you give will be the measure you get."

What we're talking about here, of course, is what some religions call *karma*. Like the biblical idea of sowing and reaping, the law of karma asserts that everything that comes to us is a result of our own thoughts and actions — that we create our own reality, in other words.

And we can change that reality by the choices we make.

---

## Since we create our own reality, we can change it by the choices we make.

---

The bottom line is that it's to our advantage to make choices based on Love rather than fear (remember that, as we've said, these are the only two choices available).

One could say that learning to manage our karma in this way is what we bought into when we chose life on the earthly plane.

But that's quite a different way of explaining human dysfunction than attributing it to the guilt-producing fiction of 'sin'.

The way to overcome what we may perceive to be our 'sins' is to make better choices, and by so doing, create a preferable reality for ourselves.

But the idea of sin as such is nothing but a red herring.

So you could say that if we believe in sin, our only real 'sin' is that we believe in sin!

---

**If we believe in sin, our only real 'sin' is that we believe in sin!**

---

# THERE IS NO DEATH

Another popular idea that does us no good is belief in death.

While it's true that our bodies die (thank goodness!), since we're only using them temporarily that really has nothing to do with it.

The truth is that we all live forever, whether we like it or not!

As for life on earth, many people in our culture think we live in an earthly body only once. Others believe we experience as many lifetimes as it takes for us to achieve enlightenment (i.e. replacing fear with Love) and that even Jesus had to do this.

If we find the idea of reincarnation serviceable — in giving meaning to inequities of birth, for example — it can be a helpful concept. Yet in our tradition it remains only an option. And that's OK, since all we really need to know about this is that life is continuous.

But regardless of our beliefs about earthly life, the human body remains only an interim communication device; no more, no less. The truth is that we inhabit bodies only in order to learn that living in bodies doesn't work as an alternative to living consciously as part of God.

---

**Living in bodies doesn't work as an alternative to living consciously as part of God.**

---

So, when we talk about 'death', what we're really talking about is a specific rite of passage.

But death itself is nothing at all.

# WE HAVE NO NEED FOR 'SALVATION'

The fact that there is no sin means that there's really no need for 'salvation'.

If there's no sin, what would we be 'saved' from?

For example, the idea that we need to be saved from hell is a bill of goods. There *is* no hell (other than the private one we may appear to make through various forms of selfishness).

Hell is a purely human fabrication and it doesn't exist. Only what God creates exists, and God creates only by extending Love, remember?

By no stretch of the imagination could what we call 'hell' be an extension of Love. In fact, the idea of hell is a human attempt to invent an extension of the opposite of Love, which is fear.

Fear is nothing more than faith in evil, and God didn't create that, either.

---
# Fear is nothing more than faith in evil.
---

And, by the way, there's no such thing as a 'devil' or Satan, though it's OK to make jokes about these guys. In fact, that's the best thing to do with this hilarious idea.

Having said all this, however, there's one thing we do need to be saved from – and that's our ignorance.

That's where Jesus comes in. It's true that 'Jesus saves' because he can save us from our ignorance. That was his function 2000 years ago; that's his function today.

The only difference is that we now know far more about his message than the people of his time did.

For example, some of the people of Jesus' time (including, unfortunately, some of the people who helped to write the texts which eventually found their way into what we now call the Bible) thought that Jesus' death somehow saved them from the effects of sin. That's nonsense – it did no such thing. According to Dominic Crossan, a Roman Catholic theologian, this mistaken belief is "the most unfortunately successful idea in the history of Christian thought"!

One more point: the fact that Jesus can and does save us from our ignorance in no way suggests that he's the only teacher who can do this. There have been many others, and there are some today.

This book is oriented towards Jesus and his teachings. But that's just a bias.

# THERE IS NOTHING
# TO FORGIVE

The way Jesus saves us from our ignorance is really quite simple.

In fact, the only thing we actually need to know about his message is that it's a message of forgiveness.

But if there is no sin, what is there to forgive?

The obvious answer is: *nothing*!

To believe that there is actually something to forgive is to believe in attack, guilt, fear and death.

But as Jesus demonstrated through the extreme example of his own 'death' and resurrection, none of these things is real.

That is the secret of forgiveness as taught by Jesus.

There is nothing to forgive!

But if there is nothing to forgive, why do it?

Again, the answer is quite simple: forgiveness is the ultimate healing therapy, both for us, and for the world.

The reason for that is that forgiveness gives us everything we want and everything the world needs.

And it always works (there are no exceptions to this).

It works for us because it gives us inner peace.

It works for the world because when we have peace within ourselves, the world gets healed automatically.

So we do it out of what you might call enlightened self-interest.

But *how* do we forgive if there's nothing to forgive?

The answer to that riddle is that we forgive precisely in order to learn that there's nothing to forgive!

This may sound simple, and it is. But that doesn't mean it's easy.

What makes it hard to do is that in order for our forgiveness to be real, it has to be *unconditional.*

And it can only be unconditional if we let go of our judgements.

And that's the toughest thing we'll ever have to do in this world.

---

**Forgiveness is the ultimate healing therapy, both for us, and for the world.**

---

# REDISCOVERING JESUS

*… meeting Jesus again for the first time.*
**Marcus Borg**

# PROLOGUE

To rediscover Jesus can be to rediscover life.

But which Jesus?

The biblical scholarship of the past 300 years has helped us to find out by blowing the whistle on some of the trivial understandings of scripture that have bedeviled Christianity in past centuries.

Among other things, this has helped us to bring our portrait of Jesus into sharper focus.

Yet despite some new discoveries, the source material with which biblical scholars have had to work remains limited and their efforts to reveal the real Jesus are inevitably inconclusive and open-ended.

In fact, as R.H. Lightfoot, a prominent New Testament scholar of the last century, famously put it at the conclusion of a Bampton Lecture delivered at Oxford in 1934: "[the gospels] yield us little more than a whisper of his voice; we trace in them but the outskirts of his ways."

If this is so, who is the Jesus we can hope to rediscover?

It is to this question that the third section of this little book is addressed.

# DETACHING JESUS FROM CHRISTIANITY

The first step in rediscovering Jesus is to disconnect him from Christianity.

By 'Christianity' we mean a Jesus-inspired offshoot of Judaism that split off towards the end of the first century C.E. and began to gel as a discrete belief system in the Mediterranean world of the fourth century.

This belief system became the official religion of the Roman Empire after the Emperor Constantine used it as a means of consolidating his political power.

Under Constantine's influence, Christianity began to be defined by its official creeds, notably the Nicene Creed, which was developed in its initial form during the early part of the fourth century. (This creed takes its name from the fact that the first general conference of Christian bishops, which launched the process of developing it, met in what is now Turkey at a place called Nicea – known today as Iznik.)

The Nicene Creed is still in widespread public use. Even churches that don't include it in their liturgies are likely to uphold the belief system it presents, so it can still serve as a broad and succinct statement of Christian belief.

The Nicene Creed can be summed up as follows:

1) As its name suggests, the key belief that sets Christianity apart from other religions is that Jesus of Nazareth was in fact 'the Christ', by which is meant that he was both human and divine and, as such, "the only Son of God".

2) Following on from this is the unique belief that Jesus was sent by God to save the world, primarily through his sacrificial death on the Cross, which is seen to be the means of our salvation through the forgiveness of sins, as realized in Baptism.

3) After his death, the authenticity of Jesus's mission was confirmed by means of a number of resurrection appearances.

4) At that time, his followers also experienced the reality of the God Jesus had affirmed through a dynamic presence that came to be known as the "Holy Spirit".

5) They likewise came to believe that Jesus would return or "come again".

In disconnecting Jesus from this belief system, it is only necessary to delete the first *two* of these ideas.

The remaining three points retain validity, regardless of the extent to which they are identified as 'Christian'.

## Some of the ideas in the Nicene Creed are quite valid.

# JESUS IS ONE OF US

There has been much confusion about the identity of Jesus of Nazareth and what it might mean for us today.

This confusion has been largely caused by the fact that in the fourth century the Church committed itself to the impossible proposition that Jesus was uniquely both human and divine and, as such, the "only Son of God". (As an Anglican bishop once observed, such a theory would have astonished the first Christians!)

It should be obvious that as it stands, this idea, which is known as the doctrine of the Incarnation, is logically insupportable (like trying to mix oil and water). So it's not surprising that there have been many attempts to refine it. Since these second opinions have inevitably embraced the humanity of Jesus at the expense of his divinity, or vice versa, the Church has called them 'heresy' (departures from official teaching).

The sources of this confusion are two-fold:

1) The belief that the human body of Jesus was as real as his divine nature.
2) The belief that Jesus was unique.

Neither of these ideas is true.

The truth is that, as we have said, all human bodies (including that of Jesus) are nothing more than temporary communication devices.

The truth is that, while it is correct to say that God has only one "Son", that Sonship is a shared identity that includes everyone who has ever lived on earth, or who will do so in the future.

The truth is that there is therefore nothing we can say about Jesus that isn't true of all of us.

If this is so, why is Jesus so important?

What makes Jesus important is that while the Sonship of which we are a part exists only as potential in us, Jesus is one who has fully realized his identity as a Son of God. He is therefore in a position to help us as we struggle to realize that same identity within ourselves.

The only difference between Jesus and us is that he has completed the process of learning who he is, while we have not.

---

**The only difference between Jesus and us is that he has completed the process of learning who he is.**

---

In every respect, therefore, he is our brother – nothing more, nothing less.

Admittedly, he is what you might call an elder brother.

So it's OK to call him 'Lord' if we want to.

# HIS IS NOT THE
# ONLY PATH

Realizing that Jesus is one of us allows us to make another discovery: hearing his message and responding to it is not the only way to find God.

Don't let anyone ever tell you that the way of Jesus is the only true path.

That's a terrible idea, as Jesus himself knows full well.

In fact, this is just the kind of nonsense that he would save us from in the first place!

Of course, saying this doesn't mean we can't give Jesus a primary place in our own lives if we choose to do so, as long as we allow others the same courtesy when it comes to their attraction to Buddha or Mohammed, etc.

So it's never necessary to argue with others about religion. The truth is that there have been many teachers and avatars throughout history and there are obviously many paths to God.

Thus it's not up to us to try to impose our way upon others, even if we believe our path to God may be the best.

In fact, it's not necessary to believe in Jesus at all if we choose not to – he has no ego problem with that.

But as we said earlier, this book is biased towards him and there's a good reason for that: many of the distortions, contradictions and cruelties that have wracked western society can be associated with the belief system known as 'Christianity' that arose in the fourth century C.E.

Today we need to divest ourselves of these distortions and contradictions, replacing them with what one of the biblical writers called "the truth as it is in Jesus".

This short book is intended to help people to begin that process.

The process itself is likely to take some time because Christianity is now so deeply entrenched in world culture. Worse, it's still being used to justify racism, sexism, hatred and war, along with injustice and other forms of irrationality (e.g. discrimination in matters of gender orientation and practice).

Fortunately, we're getting a lot of help from Jesus himself as we move on from Christianity in our return to him. (More on that in the final chapter of this section.)

While we're working at it, there's a little rule of thumb we can apply to every situation: try a little kindness.

---

**There's a little rule of thumb we can apply to every situation: try a little kindness.**

---

This will always make the world a better place.

And it's also a good way to speed up our return to Jesus.

# THE DEATH OF JESUS WAS A NON-EVENT

One of the keys to rediscovering Jesus is to stop emphasizing his death.

Admittedly, by the world's standards, the crucifixion of Jesus was particularly cruel and harsh. That was its purpose. Jesus lived in the Roman Empire of the first century C.E. and during that period crucifixion was one way the Empire dealt with people who stepped out of line or who were deemed to be a threat.

But regardless of the circumstances in which it occurs, death is always a non-event, and the death of Jesus is no exception.

Death can never be anything but a non-event, because it can only happen to bodies, and although on this plane we are using bodies they can, as we've said, be no more than temporary communication devices.

This was as true for Jesus of Nazareth as it is for the rest of us.

The first followers of Jesus did not realize this, so they tended to emphasize the importance of the body. Accordingly, when Jesus' body was crucified by the Romans, they assumed that he was dead.

Although they changed their minds about this after Jesus later demonstrated that he was still alive, they nevertheless felt a need to explain why he (as God's 'chosen one') had 'died' in the first place.

The answer they came up with was that the crucifixion was all part of God's plan of salvation, as confirmed by the Hebrew scriptures. The way this was supposed to work was that the sacrificial death of Jesus somehow paid the penalty for human sin and made us right with God again.

Aside from the fact that this idea is totally illogical, it's also blasphemous, since it makes God a jerk!

As a kind of footnote to this insane idea, the first followers of Jesus went on to assume that unless they, too, were willing to "take up the cross" and suffer martyrdom for Jesus' cause, they weren't really being loyal to his memory.

While one can perhaps understand why they felt this way (at a time when it was actually dangerous to be identified with the Jesus movement), the fact that this idea found its way into the Bible has had the unfortunate effect of convincing many that we're not really doing our stuff for Jesus unless some kind of suffering is involved.

But God does not will suffering; God wills only joy (Love and joy are the same thing, by the way).

---

## God does not will suffering; God wills only joy.

---

What, then, is the meaning of the death of Jesus?

The answer is simple: *nothing*.

The death of Jesus has no meaning because death has no meaning.

The sole purpose of the crucifixion was in fact to exemplify this, while demonstrating unconditional love and forgiveness by the most powerful means available.

We can always be deeply grateful to Jesus for his willingness to validate these truths by means of such an extreme example.

But to call his death a real event has the effect of ignoring the demonstration and devaluing his noble achievement.

# THE RESURRECTION OF JESUS REALLY HAPPENED

Without his resurrection, we would probably never have heard of Jesus of Nazareth or 'Christianity'.

So far as we can tell, it was only the resurrection appearances that could have put the Jesus movement back on track after he was murdered by the Romans.

Or did the men and women who had followed Jesus in the flesh just make it all up after the crucifixion, as some have suggested?

That would be hard to sustain, since the narrative accounts of the resurrection we find in the gospels are too shambolic to have been contrived!

Practically speaking, it also seems doubtful that the followers of Jesus would have been so bold in promoting his cause after the crucifixion without a dramatic development of this kind (no matter how inadequately it came to be described later).

In fact, when it comes to the resurrection of Jesus, scepticism is likely to present more of a challenge than belief.

If we're unsure about it all, though, perhaps it's best to agree with the Scottish bishop who summarized the situation quite clearly by saying (of the witnesses to the resurrection) that they simply "saw what they needed to see".

The trouble begins when we try to be overly specific about what we think it is they may have seen.

For example, the bishops of the fourth century made the mistake of insisting on a belief that the resurrection of Jesus was a *bodily event.*

What they failed to realize is that the body of Jesus was of no intrinsic value (even assuming it could somehow have been reified after its death).

What's important about the resurrection of Jesus is that it demonstrated the fact that since life continues after the body dies, death has no meaning.

But it's important to realize that this would still be the case if Jesus had never lived.

The reason for that is that Jesus did not inaugurate the truth that there is no death; he simply demonstrated it.

It's also desirable to realize that there is nothing unnatural or miraculous about what we think of as 'resurrection'.

You could in fact think of it as simply a step towards the restoration of our natural state.

---

**What we call 'resurrection' is simply a step towards the restoration of our natural state.**

---

Like all life after 'death', resurrection appearances (and there have been many throughout history) are simply signs that remind us of our true nature.

They remind us of the fact that it is our nature to live forever, regardless of what may be going on (or not going on) in our current bodies at any particular moment.

# THE SECOND COMING IS A REAL EVENT

The final misperception of Jesus that we may need to correct has to do with what has been called his 'Second Coming'.

The belief that Jesus would "come again in glory to judge the living and the dead" arose initially among the first Christians. Part of the mythology that evolved around their memories of Jesus was that it seemed inconceivable that he would not return in triumph to finally put things right, and that this would happen while they were still alive.

In time, this expectation naturally subsided, and its continuation as a feature of orthodoxy has become largely symbolic.

Nevertheless, the idea that Jesus would someday return "in glory" has been revived from time to time. It has been especially prominent during the past 100 years in the United States, where it has become immensely popular, primarily through various misunderstandings of the book of Revelation.

This phenomenon has had the unfortunate effect of debasing the powerful myth of the Second Coming and allowing it to be trivialized by unsophisticated believers.

It is the thesis of the present book that the notion of the Second Coming can be given timely new relevance by a recognition that Jesus has in fact returned in our generation.

---

## Jesus has in fact returned in our generation.

---

Such a recognition rests, however, on an essential qualifier: instead of returning in visible human form, Jesus has done so in a way in which his teaching cannot now be misunderstood: in the form of a channeled document that is about the size of the Old Testament.

Because of this we need no longer focus on his human form. Instead, and for the first time in history, we can gain access to his *mind.*

The document is known as ***A Course in Miracles.***

This is not the place to embark on a detailed examination of the Course – there are now many books and websites devoted to the subject and since it was published over 30 years ago, the Course itself has been translated into 18 languages and this work is continuous.

Suffice it to say that the Course teachings, as one might expect in light of their source, are both radical and gentle: they are radical in that they challenge virtually every perception of reality that we hold; they are gentle in that they allow us to move gradually beyond our false perceptions to truth, and to do so in practical and manageable increments.

To those who would pursue the Course teachings, however, a word of caution may be in order: while they are both radical and gentle, they are also life-changing.

In short, they have the capacity to awaken us from the dream of Christianity to "the Truth as it is in Jesus".

Whether they will yet be able to do this on a widespread scale remains in doubt, given what is bound to be strong resistance from those entrenched in and defensive of Christianity. (Some estimates of the length of time required for a widespread acceptance of the Course teachings range from 200 to 500 years!)

Meanwhile, however, the Course is being quietly absorbed by millions of readers and there are local study groups and larger Course-oriented gatherings all over the world.

One can only hope that as these students awaken, they will in turn become teachers of the Course's message of love and forgiveness.

# FROM CHRISTIANITY TO CHRISTHOOD

*"Forget your dreams of sin and guilt, and
come with me instead
to share the resurrection of God's Son."*
**A Course in Miracles**

# FROM CHRISTIANITY TO CHRISTHOOD

The function of form is to serve as a vehicle for content.

All religion consists of form.

Thus all religion is, as the saying goes, a 'movable feast', though the content that it aims to represent, which is common to many religions, is not.

When a given religious form begins to unravel as a functional vehicle for content, it needs to be superseded.

Such is the case with Christianity in the 21$^{st}$ century: this form can no longer serve as a vehicle for the content of the message of Jesus.

In passing it might be said that at this stage we do not need to concern ourselves with senseless musings about the Christianity of the past. While it could be argued that the Christianity our culture inherited from the Church of the fourth century has *never* been adequately reflective of the mind of Jesus, that is not our concern here. Our present purpose is solely to encourage the replacement of the dysfunctional Christianity of *today*.

Although many attempts have been made to revitalize Christianity, until now we have not been able to replace it (though happily, some contemporary biblical scholarship has helped to pave the way).

Yet moving on from today's confused 'Christianity' is the only thing that will really work in the present situation.

Providentially, with the coming of *A Course in Miracles*, we are able, for the first time ever, to do this, and to do it with safe assurance.

Today, in fact, the human race can have direct access to the mind of Jesus, who alone has the authority to oversee the replacement of the religious form that has been associated with him.

What this means, in practical terms applicable to the message of Jesus, is that it is now possible to make the transition (in the Course Jesus prefers the word "transfer") from form to content.

Though this transfer is presented to us in the form of a thought system, the goal of its curriculum is in fact far broader: the ultimate purpose of the Course is a shared return to the memory of God, Who is our common Source.

In this respect, it could be said that the path that lies before us is one leading from Christianity to a recognition of the Christhood we all share collectively as 'the Son of God'.

Jesus has returned to show us the way.

---

## Jesus has returned to show us the way.

---

We need but follow.

# POSTSCRIPT

One of the primary aims of the progressive biblical scholarship of the past three centuries has been to differentiate (in due course) between the ministry of Jesus and the belief system that arose in its aftermath, which subsequently came to be identified as biblical and credal Christianity. Although the latter has claimed Jesus as its inspiration and focus, it also reflects later historical and personal influences that have had the effect of diluting and corrupting the dominical gospel.

While much progress has been made towards attaining this goal, particularly in recent years, full success has remained essentially beyond reach. With the coming of **A Course in Miracles**, however, the task has at last been achieved. We have rediscovered Jesus and we can now upgrade to "the truth as it is in Jesus".

Although they retain the Trinitarian structure of conventional Christianity, as well as much of its terminology, the Course teachings differ from those of orthodoxy in their concept of God, the role of Jesus and the function of the Holy Spirit. They restore us to an awareness of a full identity with God that reflects only Love and which is therefore free of all traces of fear, guilt and belief in separation. Though the main body of the Course is characterized by abstract (though contemporary) language, this is accompanied by a simpler workbook section that enables the student to apply the teachings to daily life in manageable segments. A final section is in question and answer form.

As might be expected, these teachings are powerfully transformative.

For more information about the Course, the following websites are recommended:

http://www.acim.org/ (Foundation for Inner Peace)

http://www.facim.org/ (Foundation for *A Course in Miracles*)

For information about Course study groups worldwide:

http://www.miraclecenter.org/ (Miracle Distribution Center)

# SUGGESTED READING

*A Course in Miracles\** (Text, Workbook, Manual for Teachers)
*The Song of Prayer: Prayer, Forgiveness, Healing\** (An Extension of the Principles of *A Course in Miracles*)

\* Both books are available from any book seller or from The Foundation for Inner Peace, P.O. Box 598, Mill Valley CA 94942-0598, U.S.A. (http://www.acim.org/)

Please note that with the recent release of the Third Edition of the Course (2007), both books are now available in a single volume. (They include an explanation of what the Course is, what it says and how it came.)

(*So far the Course has been translated into 18 languages, and additional translations are in progress.*)

6611576R0

Made in the USA
Charleston, SC
13 November 2010